Clifton Smith

The illustrated and historical souvenir of Central park, with

indexed map

Vol. 1

Clifton Smith

The illustrated and historical souvenir of Central park, with indexed map
Vol. 1

ISBN/EAN: 9783337806613

Printed in Europe, USA, Canada, Australia, Japan

Cover: Foto ©ninafisch / pixelio.de

More available books at **www.hansebooks.com**

THE

ILLUSTRATED and HISTORICAL

SOUVENIR of CENTRAL PARK,

WITH INDEXED MAP.

✥

PUBLISHED BY

WM. F. SMITH & CO.,

10 EAST 14TH ST., N. Y.

COPYRIGHT 1893, BY C. O. SMITH.

Printers:
J. W. PRATT & SON.

Engravers:
N. Y. ENGRAVING & PTG. CO.

LAKE NEAR...

CONTENTS.

The MAP shows
at a glance how to
REACH and SEE every
OBJECT of INTEREST.

5

ENTRAL PARK, one of the most beautiful in the world, was, within the memory of the present generation, a waste of rock and swamp, offering no suggestion of its present charm, and sufficiently uninviting and rugged in its aspect to discourage the most enthusiastic engineer. Since then a paradise has been created by an outlay of upwards of $14,000,-000. The conformation of Manhattan Island afforded but slight natural advantages for the creation of a great park. Geologically it is described as "a long, narrow tongue of rock, chiefly gneiss and mica-schists contorted and upturned at every angle." In the crevices of these rocks natural springs and decaying vegetation had formed forbidding pools and swamps. Over all this, the great glacial drift had scattered its boulders, and smooth rounded and grooved every outcrop. These external evidences of world-making have been entirely effaced in the Southern portion of the city, but enough of them remain in the Northern part to indicate the roughness and ruggedness of the area out of which the authorities undertook to create Central Park. After considerable necessary preliminary preparation, the work was actually commenced in 1857, the landscape design being by Frederick Law Olmstead and Calvert Vaux, and the architecture by Mr. Vaux, assisted by J. W. Mould. Not only had the impression which Nature in her wildest mood had left upon the earth's surface to be utilized or removed in the formation of this great park, but forests had to be reproduced and a new mantle of verdure spread over all. Barren commons were to be converted into lawns and meadows of perennial beauty, swamps turned into pellucid lakes and roads constructed everywhere, regardless of obstacles. But the genius and skill of man, backed by the wealth of a great city, were equal to the task, and a single generation served to see the "waste places made glad, and the wilderness blossom like the rose," and to-day the completed park stands forth a most striking monument of the skill of engineers and landscape architects, and may be spoken of now as a finished work, taking on new beauties and adding to its attractions from season to season. All the work of construction and maintenance is done under the direction of the Department of Public Parks. The Board of Commissioners are: President, George C. Clausen; Vice-President, Abraham B. Tappen; Nathan Straus and Edward Bell, Commissioners; Charles De F. Burns, Secretary; Samuel Parsons, Jr., Superintendent of Parks; M. A. Kellogg, Engineer of Construction; Captain of Police, C. C. Collins.

The Park embraces an area of 840 acres, extending from 59th to 110th St., and from 5th to 8th Aves. In length it is a little more than 2½ miles, and in width it exceeds half a mile. Its surface is composed of 653¾ acres of land and 185¾ acres of water—the latter being made up by two reservoirs covering 142 acres, and a series of beautiful lakes and ponds, aggregating 43¾ acres. Nearly 9 miles of drives, of an average width of 54 feet—the widest being 60 feet—traverse it; the bridle paths, 16½ feet wide, extend 5½ miles, and the walks, 16 feet wide, 28¼ miles.

Bridges and Archways.—There are 36 in the Park, which are more or less ornamental, and no two are alike. There are 12 tunnels, constructed to screen the sunken roadways

LAKE AND BOW BRIDGE

which traverse the Park on the lines of 65th, 79th, 85th and 97th Sts. The wooded ground covers about 400 acres, on which have been planted more than half a million trees, shrubs and vines, and the meadows and lawns spread their velvet smoothness over many acres. Seats are provided for 10,000 people, 600 of which are in vine-covered arbors. There are 30 buildings within the Park. Five or six are for the accommodation of the public.

Park Carriages are provided for visitors desiring to see the larger portion of the Park and many of its attractive features without fatigue, and are located at the entrances at 5th and 8th Aves. and 59th St. The fare for the entire trip is 25 cents.

The Drives.—Stretching for more than two miles through the center of Manhattan Island, with two of the principal avenues interrupted by its expanse, and two others skirting its entire length, the Park is easily accessible from all directions. It is beautiful all the year round, but is particularly so in the early Spring. It is at all times the fashionable drive, and every afternoon an unending cavalcade pours in at the 5th Ave. entrance, composed mainly of superbly appointed family equipages. Owners of fast horses more often drive up Broadway, and, passing in at the 8th Ave. entrance, proceed through the park to Central Ave., beyond the Harlem River.

Metropolitan Museum of Art.—First among the attractions of the Park is this grand temple, devoted to the collection and preservation of works which mark the world's progress-ive epochs in taste and refinement, and to the dissemination of knowledge that will assist humanity to an appreciation of the endeavors of men in ages past, and thus become a great factor in raising the standard of civilization. The Museum of Art was founded less than a quarter of a century ago by philanthropic citizens, and when the fact is considered that it

Metropolitan Museum of Art.

has never been helped or aided (except to a limited extent, and that not bestowed upon its collection) by governmental munificence, its progress has been truly wonderful. In that brief period it has gathered within its walls treasures which, in many respects, rival the collections of the most famous museums of Europe. The institution was chartered by the State "for the purpose of establishing a Museum and Library of Art; of encouraging and developing the study of the fine arts; of the application of Art to manufactures and to private life; of advancing the general knowledge of kindred subjects, and to that end, of furnishing popular instruction and recreation." It is governed by a board of twenty-one Trustees, in addition to whom the Comptroller of the City of New York, the President of the Department of Public Parks and the President of the National Academy of Design are *ex-officio* members. Officers of the Corporation for the year ending 1894: President, Henry G. Marquand; Vice-Presidents, F. W. Rhinelander, D. Huntington; Treasurer, Hiram Hitchcock; Secretary, L. P. di Cesnola. The contribution of $50,000 to the funds of the Museum confers upon the donor the title of Benefactor; of $5,000 to election as a Patron, or Fellow in perpetuity; of $1,000 to election as a Fellow for life. Contributions of works of art to the value of twice these amounts may be accepted instead of cash payments. Honorary Fellows for life may be elected by the Trustees. Patrons and fellows enjoy all the privileges the Museum affords in the way of study, and are also entitled to a certain number of tickets, transferable to others, and admitting the holder to the exhibitions, at all times. The connection of the Museum with the Park is this: In consideration of the accommodations furnished by the city, the Trustees admit the public free of charge on Tuesdays, Wednesdays, Thursdays, Saturdays, Sunday afternoons, holidays,

and on Monday and Friday evenings, beside certain privileges accorded to instructors, students, schools, etc. Mondays and Fridays 25 cents is charged.

Invited by the city to remove the Museum to the Park, the Trustees accepted; the city agreeing to provide a building and contribute to the equipment and maintenance. By law a plot of ground was set apart and transferred to the use of the Museum for its buildings, east of the old receiving reservoir, and bounded on the East by Fifth Avenue, South by the continuation of Eightieth Street, West by the drive, North by the continuation of Eighty-fifth Street, and comprising eighteen and one-half acres. This plot it is intended eventually to fill with the building and its extensions. The city expended in erecting the building now occupied by the Museum nearly two million dollars; the accommodations being increased from time to time as the growth of the institution required. The Museum was removed to the Park in 1879, and on the 30th of March, 1880, was formally opened by the President of the United States. The first acquisition of any importance made by the Museum was the Blodgett collection of paintings, consisting mainly of examples of Flemish and Dutch masters, but containing also some fair specimens of French, Spanish and English art. Next came the archæological collection made in Cyprus by General di Cesnola. These accumulations were followed by smaller but equally valuable specimens, so that when it removed to the home provided for it in the Park a fair indication of its destined greatness was apparent. Since then, and particularly in the last few years, munificent donations from citizens of New York have increased its treasures to their present grand proportions, and scarcely a month now passes without a valuable donation being made to it. Entering the building at the South, in front of the visitor may be found some excellent modern sculpture, and to the right

14

Metropolitan Museum of Art.

15

Egyptian antiquities, among which are sarcophagi and mummies. Ancient terra cottas are seen to the North, and antique sculpture, bronzes and inscriptions follow these. To the left, on entering from the Park, is the hall of glass, laces and pottery, relative to which says a worthy authority: "It is doubtful if any other museum in the world can equal this illustration of the history of glass." The McCullum, Stuart and Astor laces, of rarest design and exquisite tracery, showing in many examples the most delicate webs ever woven by human fingers, are very beautiful, and naturally of great value. These are arranged so as to be seen to advantage and without danger of injury. Near these are collections of musical instruments as comprehensive as they are curious, and to which numerous additions are soon to be made and rearranged. Passing on through this section we come upon collections of bronze statues, and figures (which, however, are soon to be rearranged in another hall) of intricate wrought-iron work, of precious antiquities in many strangely designed forms, until we arrive at the lofty hall in which are erected accurate models of the Parthenon, Notre Dame and other noted ancient buildings. Conspicuous on the West wall is hung Makart's colossal painting, "Diana's Hunting Party," and on the East Constant's "Emperor Justinian."

Leaving the agreeable atmosphere of this storied locality we soon gain access to the upper halls, where the eye and mind will be engrossed with the contributions of palaces, churches and private collections of the Old World. Here every nook and corner is enriched with choice accumulations, about which the catalogues, in a measure, enlighten the earnest visitor. The painters of the great schools of all nations and times, old and modern masters, fill the many galleries and awaken the most varied sentiments of the student. A rather hasty glance reveals a vast number of notable pictures, chief among

16

Museum of Art.

17

them being (15) Léon Bonnat's "Egyptian Fellah, Woman and Child;" (22) Constant Troyou's "Holland Cattle;" (52) Pierre Cot's "The Storm;" (112) Gabriel Max's "The Last Token;" (117) Alex. Cabanel's "The Shulammite;" (124) Ludwig Knaus' "The Holy Family;" all of which are in the Wolfe collection. In Gallery V is (186) Rosa Bonheur's "The Horse Fair;" (220) Fortuny's "A Spanish Lady;" (242) Edouard Detaille's "The Defence of Champigny;" (216) J. L. E. Meissonier's "Friedland, 1807." Gallery Y : (24) Peter Paul Rubens' "Return of the Holy Family from Egypt;" (51) Vandyck's "St. Martha Interceding with God for a Cessation of the Plague at Tarascon;" (58) Jacob Jordaens' "The Visit of St. John to the Infant Jesus;" (95) Greuze's "Study of a Head;" (5) Sir Joshua Reynolds' "Large Portrait Group," three small figures. In the Marquand Gallery (34) Rubens' "Susanna and the Elders;" (37) Rembrandt's "Portrait of a Man;" (39) Gainsborough's "Girl With a Cat;" (40) Turners' "Saltash;" (46) Vandyck's "Duke of Richmond;" (45 & 47) Constable's "A Lock on the Stour" and "The Valley Farm;" (14) Franz Hals' "Portrait of a Woman."

In other galleries adjacent one may study the wonderful creations in Gobelin tapestries, bequeathed by the late Elizabeth V. Coles; vases of bronze, malachites, marble, enamels; statuettes in terra-cotta, found in Tanagra, so human and artistic in pose and grace; volumes of photographs of Renaissance Italian work; glass, pottery, fragments of statuary; wall stucco, frescoes and mosaics; engravings, prints, manuscripts; Babylonian seals and cylinders, now the finest collection in the world, save that of the British Museum, and which, with additions soon to be arranged, will be the most extensive and comprehensive extant. The Gold and Silver Gallery of the North wing will be three times the dimensions of that of the South wing, and unsurpassed both in rarity and excellence

18

of examples displayed, as well as the method of exposing this beautiful and educational exhibit; so also the series of rooms in the new wing, each in their charming way, will be found replete both in floor and wall cases with objects beautiful and instructive to contemplate. In addition to what has been mentioned the visitor will discover in a mosaic by Rinaldi, "Ruins of Pæstum," a work of marvelous execution; and the Oriental porcelains, as well as the collections of Assyrian, Babylonian, Egyptian antiquities, and of pre-historic American antiquities, will elicit profound admiration.

In the space allotted to the Museum of Art in this work can be given only an epitome of its vast values. The Cyprus Collection alone, unearthed by Gen. L. P. di Cesnola, and which has no parallel anywhere for extent and variety, would, with its stone sculptures, sarcophagi, inscriptions, alabastra, ivories, lamps, pottery, terra-cotta statuettes, bronzes, glass, gems, jewelry and other objects in gold and silver; Assyrian, Egyptian, Phœnician, Greek and Roman in character, and of other dates from the earliest times to later than the Christian era, form a unique, distinctive and important museum. Every day this collection is becoming more and more precious by the comparative light of new discoveries giving it a completeness quite inestimable. It has made Homer more comprehensive, it has enlightened the world upon facts which, previous to its discovery, were not dreamed of. Truly the American people, if they are not to-day grateful in their possession of this Collection, will, at no distant day, rise up and glorify the zeal and ardor of its worthy discoverer.

The Museum's collection of glass was increased by a purchase from Charvet, by Henry G. Marquand, and by him presented to the Museum; also a later collection gathered by the late James Jackson Jarves, making the entire collection of glass the richest and most valu-

19

able known. Of other collections of note the following may well be mentioned as being exceptionally fine: the Huntington memorials of Washington, Franklin and Lafayette; the E. C. Moore ancient terra-cotta statuettes (Tanagra and Myrina), ancient and mediæval glass, Oriental enameled and other pottery, and objects of art in metal, ivory, etc.; the Lazarus miniatures, enamels, jewelry and fans, the Drexel objects of art in gold and silver, the C. W. King collection of ancient gems, purchased and presented to the Museum by John Taylor Johnston; the Oriental porcelains acquired from S. P. Avery; the Japanese swords purchased at the sale of the Ives collection; the musical instruments of all nations, presented by Mrs. John Crosby Brown, with a smaller collection presented by J.W. Drexel; the Baker and other examples of ancient textile fabrics from the Fayoum in Egypt; the pictures, gold medals and other objects commemorative of the laying of the Atlantic cable, presented by the late Cyrus W. Field; the models of inventions by the late Capt. John Ericsson, presented by George H. Robinson; the reproductions of ivory carvings, exhibiting the mediæval continuance of the art, Renaissance iron work, Della Robbia altar-piece, metallic reproductions of gold and silver objects in the Imperial Russian Museum, all presented by Henry G. Marquand; the Levi H. Willard architectural casts, amounting to over $100,000 in value; the Marquand sculptural casts, the beginning of a series of casts which will illustrate progressive art from earliest examples to the later Christian; drawings by the old masters collected by Count Maggiori of Bologna, Signor Marietta, Prof. Angelini and Dr. Guastala, purchased and presented by Cornelius Vanderbilt, also another set presented by Mrs. Cephas G. Thompson; and several collections of paintings by old Dutch and Flemish masters, and others. The symmetry of the Museum thus appears no less remarkable than its growth; rendering its collections

20

Metropolitan Museum of Art

21

of untold value to the artist, artisan and art student, as well as the scholar and those who simply wander about in search of something entertaining and curious. The instructional phase of the Museum's existence is still further augmented by regular courses of lectures given on art and archæology on Saturday mornings during the winter by special arrangements with Columbia College; these features coupled with the Museum Library and other educational facilities round out the character and magnitude of one of the greatest museums in the world. Entrance, 5th Ave. and 82d St.

American Museum of Natural History.—While not in the Park, this institution is for all purposes a feature of it, being located in Manhattan Square, which adjoins the Park on the West side, extending from 77th to 81st St., and from 8th to 9th Ave. A stone bridge connects the building occupied by the Museum with the Park at 77th St., so that communication between the two is uninterrupted. The Natural History Museum was founded the same year as that of the Museum of Art, and very much in the same way; the relations between it and the city are similar, and membership is secured in the same manner and at like rates; but this institution being more of a school, annual tickets are sold for $10, giving the holder all privileges for investigation and study; rooms are provided for the accommodation of students, and a regular series of lectures are delivered by competent instructors. A part of the original design of the Museum is the establishment of a post-graduate university of natural science, where students may find as complete collections and facilities as those now existing or offered in Berlin and London. The institution grows rapidly, both in aggregation and in value, and is destined to rank with the best of its kind in the world, and competent judges now accord it the pre-eminent position among similar institutions of our country. Before the Museum was

AMERICAN MUSEUM OF NATURAL HISTORY.

incorporated, many important acquisitions were secured for it, consisting of the Verreaux collection of natural history specimens; the Elliott collection of the birds of North America, and the entire Museum of Prince Maximilian of Neuwied; the money required to secure them being raised by private contributions, most of it being subscribed by the trustees—twenty-five in number—of the embryo institution. The corner-stone for the building was laid on the 2d of June, 1874, by President Grant, and the completed edifice was formally opened on the 22d of December, 1877, President Hayes being present and assisting at the ceremonies. It has progressed in public favor, and the city authorities have dealt liberally with it. Many thousands of dollars have been expended in beautifying the square in which the institution stands, and in a few years it will be surrounded by grounds comparing favorably with the Park itself. The Museum is entered from the South, and is divided into halls 170 feet long by 60 wide. The first story is largely devoted to specimens of mammalia, but contains also the Forestry Collection, presented by Morris K. Jesup, consisting of every known variety of North American woods, 512 in number. The collection also contains an excellent section of the Redwood, and a superb specimen of the Giant Sequoia (big tree) from California, the gift of C. P. Huntington, Esq.

The Geological Department compares favorably with the most important of its kind in the country. The collections of American gems and gem material exhibited in Paris, presented by J. Pierpont Morgan, has been arranged and displayed in cases specially constructed for this gift. It presents a most attractive appearance, and a more instructive illustration of the uses of gem stones than any similar collection. Among notable specimens in the department, is the large mass of copper ore from Montana, weighing

24

GEOLOGICAL HALL,

SHOWING SKELETON OF

MASTODON AND GIANT MOA.

WOOD HALL
"JESUP COLLECTION,"

AND SECTION OF

BIG TREE.

6,041 pounds, especially rich in both copper and silver, and the three large blocks of limestone from Beirut, Syria. Here also are specimens of gold and silver ore, phosphate rock; a collection of corundums—"emery ores"—and the large cube of azurite displayed in the mining exhibit of Arizona at the World's Columbian Exposition, and donated to the Museum by the Copper Queen Mining Co.

The Department of Mammals and Birds contains over 10,000 mounted birds, and a large collection of mammals, reptiles and fishes. Among these may be noted the George N. Lawrence Ornithological Collection and the Elliot Collection of Humming Birds.

The Conchological Department contains a very rare and extensive collection of shells, notable for their extreme beauty and perfection, embracing, among many others, the collections formed by the late Dr. Jay, D. Jackson Steward and John J. Crooke.

The Department of Entomology has over 350,000 specimens of insects from all parts of the globe, and is extremely rich in material from this country. The collection of butterflies and moths consists of over 60,000 specimens. The Harry Edwards, the Angus, the Elliott, and the Drexel and Grote & Robinson Collections are in this Department.

The Department of Archæology and Ethnology embraces implements of the Pacific Islanders, Indian dresses and weapons, stone weapons of American aborigines, and a similar collection from the valley of the Somme, in France; specimens from the pre-historic cliff·and lake dwellers, pottery, textile fabrics, weaving implements, mummies, sculptures and more than three hundred gold, silver and copper ornaments from the excavations of South America. Notable in this department is the widely known collection of Col. Jones, of Georgia; the Appleton Sturgis Collection from the South Sea

Islands; the Terry Collection of objects from the mound builders of the Pacific Coast, and the Bishop and Emmons Collections of Implements, etc., from Alaska.

The Department of Mammalian Palæontology, lately formed, aims to provide complete series of the fossil mammalia of North America, and at the present period the collections embrace nearly one-half of the material required. The progress made leaves but little room for doubt that the coming three years will witness the completion of this great work and provide for exhibition and study an unequaled collection.

The Library of the institution numbers over 26,000 volumes on the various branches of natural science, included in which is a rare collection of books and pamphlets relating to fish and fishing and a valuable special library on shells. The Museum is open to the public free on Wednesdays, Thursdays, Fridays, Saturdays, and Sunday afternoons, holidays, and on Tuesday and Saturday evenings. Mondays and Tuesdays 25 cents is charged.

The officers of the institution are: Morris K. Jesup, President; James M. Constable, D. Jackson Steward, Vice-Presidents; Charles Lanier, Treasurer; John H. Winser, Secretary and Assistant Treasurer; William Wallace, Superintendent of Buildings.

The Obelisk.—This wonderful monument of remotest ages stands on a mound near the Museum of Art, and is most readily reached from the entrance at 5th Ave. and 79th St. It was presented to the City of New York by the Khedive of Egypt, Ismail Pasha, in 1877, and was removed and placed in position by Commander Gorringe, of the U. S. Navy, the whole expense of its transfer and erection being defrayed by the late William H. Vanderbilt. It is a monolith of red granite, nearly 70 ft. high, and weighing about 440,000 pounds. In form it is a slightly tapering square, measuring through its base 7 ft., and terminating in a pyramidal top, which originally, it is asserted, was covered with polished copper or brass. Previous to removal it stood near Alexandria, in Egypt, on the site of the Temple of On, of which it had once been an ornament, while its mate—now standing in London—had fallen centuries before, and lay partly buried in the sand. In size it is sixth among the existing Obelisks of Egypt, but in interest it is second to none of the monuments of that wonderful people. This Obelisk was erected at the command of Thutmes III., one of the greatest of Egyptian monarchs, fully fifteen hundred years before the commencement of the Christian era, and is therefore 3,400 years old. It carries the beholder back to the period of the captivity of the Israelites. It was doubtless seen, and the inscription upon it read by Moses, who was learned in the learning of the Egyptians. It was an ancient monument when Antony and Cæsar contended for universal sovereignty and the favor of Cleopatra. The faces of the Obelisk were covered with hieroglyphic inscriptions, but those on one face are now illegible. On the apex the inscriptions date from the time of its erection, and commemorate the glory of Thutmes. They are all similar and are thus translated: "The Strong Bull, who manifests himself King in the Thebaid, the Son of the Sun: Thutmes. The Gracious God, Lord of the Two Worlds, King of Upper and Lower Egypt: Ra-men-Kheper." On the body of the Obelisk there are three inscriptions on each face, the center line being the original, and all the faces being similar. It is translated: "Horus: Magnified and Enlightened by the Crown of Upper Egypt. The King of Upper and Lower Egypt: Ra-men-Kheper. The Golden Horus. The Strong of Arm, who beat the Kings of Foreign Nations, who were numbered by hundreds of thousands; for his Father, the Sun-god Ra, ordained for him

30

EGYPTIAN
OBELISK
CENTRAL PARK
NY

31

victories over all Lands. Mighty Power was concentrated at the points of his hands to widen the boundaries of Egypt. The Son of the Sun: Thutmes. Who gives Life of all Stability and Purity to-day as ever after." The lines on each side of this center inscription were placed upon the Obelisk about three hundred years after its erection by Rameses, a descendant of Thutmes, to commemorate his victories and achievements.

The Mall is the chief promenade, nearly a quarter of a mile long and 208 ft. wide, and extends from the Marble Arch to the Terrace, bordered by double rows of American elms, with the Green on one side and a bold, rocky ridge on the other. It is paved with asphalt, and ornamented with statues of Scott, Shakespeare, Burns, Halleck, and the Beethoven bust. Near its Northern end is the Music Stand, where in summer, on Saturday and Sunday afternoons, a band discourses delightful music.

The Terrace.—This elaborate work—the designs for which were prepared by Mr. Calvert Vaux, the ornamentation being by Mr. Mould—is at the Northern end of the Mall, and leads down to the Esplanade on the shore of the Lake. A central stairway passes under the carriage road, and two side stairways are outside—the three meeting on the Esplanade. The Terrace is constructed of a very fine-grained, yellow-tinted stone, out of which are carved, for exterior ornamentation, birds, animals, fruits and flowers of wonderful beauty and intricacy. The arched roof of the central stairway, and of the hall formed by its passage under the carriage drive, is covered with brilliant tiles.

Bethesda Fountain.—This ornament of the Park stands in the Esplanade at the foot of the Terrace. It was ordered by the authorities in 1863, and ten years later was finished and put in place. Miss Emma Stebbins, of New York, designed and executed

American Museum of Natural History

33

Some Specimens in American Museum of Natural History

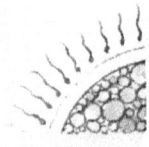

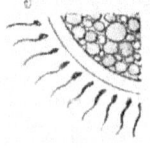

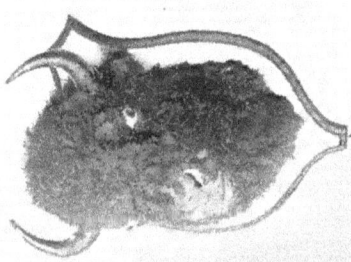

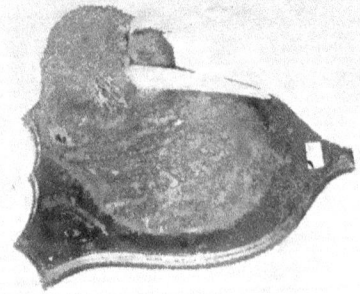

"THE MALL"
CENTRAL PARK N.Y.

35

"THE TERRACE."

34

"BETHESDA FOUNTAIN" & LAKE, CENTRAL PARK, N.Y.

35

the models in Rome, when they were sent to Munich and cast in bronze at the Royal Foundry, under the supervision of Ferdinand von Muller. The idea of the fountain was suggested by the story of the Pool of Bethesda (St. John, chapter v., verses 2-4). The figure of an angel stands in the attitude of blessing the waters which rise and move at her presence. She bears in her left hand a bunch of lilies, emblems of purity, and wears across her breast the crossed bands of the messenger-angel. She seems to hover over, as if just alighting on a mass of rock, from which the water gushes in a natural manner, falling over the edge of the upper basin, slightly veiling, but not concealing, four smaller figures, emblematic of the blessings of Temperance, Purity, Health and Peace. The figure of the angel is 8 ft. high, the upper basin is 10 ft. in diameter, and the group of four figures below are each 4 ft. high.

Statues and Monuments.—For locations and names see map.

The Dairy.—An attractive brick building situated just off the 5th Ave. Drive, near the Carousal, where a dairy lunch can be obtained at moderate price.

The Casino.—A unique stone cottage containing a restaurant, opposite the Music Stand, where you can procure all the delicacies of the season.

McGown's Pass Tavern is a fine restaurant situated on the East side of the Park near 106th St. Prices are moderate and cuisine excellent. McGown's Pass, near this tavern, is noted for several skirmishes having been fought here during the Revolutionary war. Near the Pass there are the remains of an earthwork, called Fort Fisher, that defended it; a quarter of a mile due West is the Old Fort, in a good state of preservation, also a Revolutionary relic, upon the flagstaff of which the American flag is raised upon

36

McGowan's Pass Tavern.

Casino Restaurant.

"Evacuation Day," by a descendant of the man who raised the first American flag on the staff at Bowling Green when the city was evacuated by the British army.

The Ramble lies on the hillside between the North shore of the Lake and the Old Reservoir. Here the ruggedness of Nature has been most advantageously utilized, and the result is seen in a labyrinth of winding paths leading to and through secluded nooks, shaded dells, and charming bits of scenery. Small streams dance and sparkle; miniature cascades tumble over mossy rocks, and the wanderer through these scenes could readily imagine himself many miles from a great city, so complete is the solitude, so profound are the shadows. Hidden away among the rocks here is the Cave.

Belvidere is the highest point in the Park, and located on a hill at the Southwest corner of the Old Reservoir, near the Transverse Road at 79th St. It is an open, flagged space, and contains a stone lookout tower about 50 ft. high, to which all persons are admitted. From here the Park may be seen spread like a panorama at your feet.

Reservoirs.—There are two of these vast, granite-walled structures, the old and new, covering 142 acres and containing 1,200,000,000 gallons of water. The old Reservoir is the smaller, and is in the center of the Park, between 79th and 86th Sts. The new one occupies nearly the entire breadth of the Park, between 86th and 96th Sts. Around the latter a bridle path and walk entirely surrounds it, and for equestrian exercise or promenade a more charming course could not be found anywhere.

The Menagerie.—This is located about the old Arsenal, a castellated, gray brick building, the walls of which are now almost covered by clinging ivy, which makes it very picturesque. There are many cages for animals, birds, monkeys, bear-pits, lions, tigers, bison,

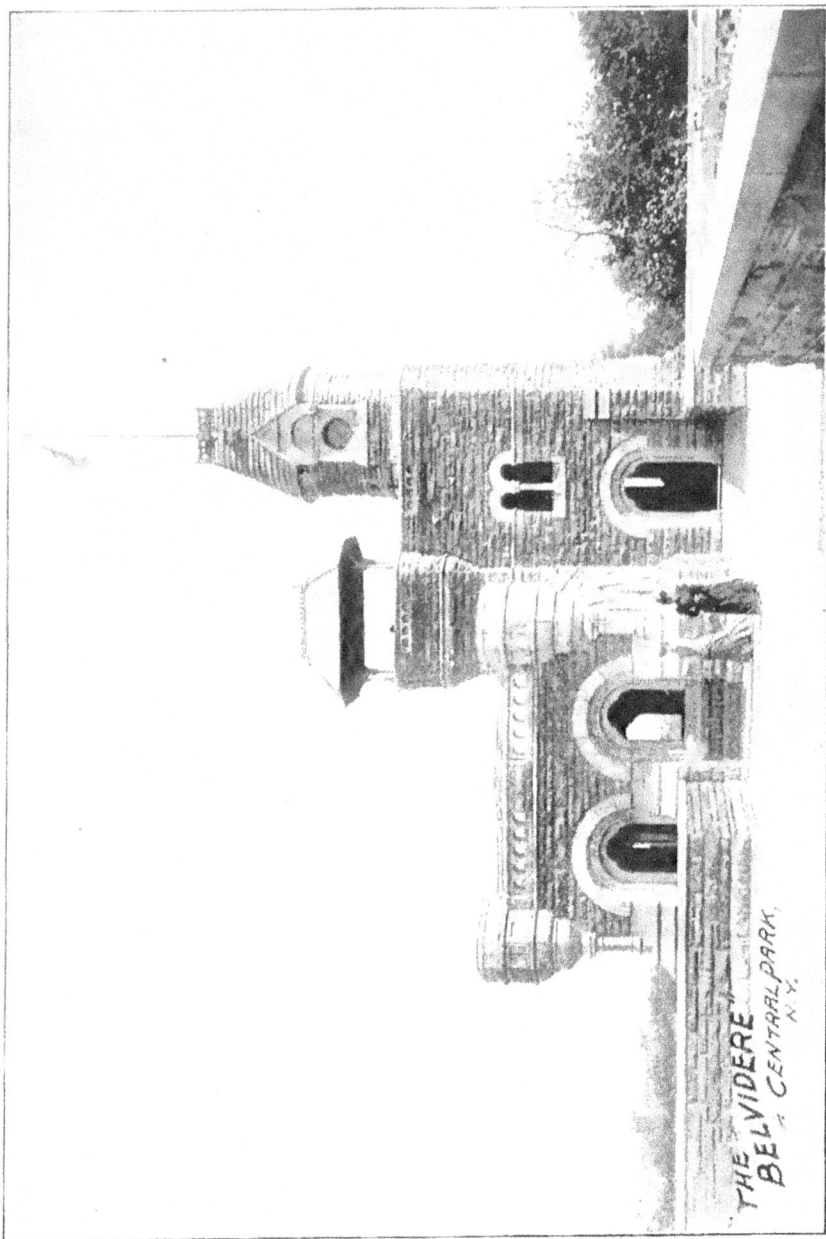

"THE BELVIDERE"
CENTRAL PARK, N. Y.

39

RIDING MEET.

41

leopards, hippopotami and other wild beasts. Entrance, 5th Ave. and 64th St.

Children's Departments.—First there is the *Carousal*, which is most readily reached from the 6th Ave. entrance at 59th St. Here swings, a merry-go-round, and plenty of room and opportunities for other amusements are provided. On the Mall are the goat carriages, and near the Menagerie are the donkeys for children to ride.

Ball Ground.—Adjoining the Carousal is a fine stretch of lawn, containing 10 acres, set apart for the use of boys who desire to play base-ball or cricket, or parties for croquet or lawn-tennis. Nearest entrance, 59th St. and 7th Ave.

The Green is a fine meadow of 16 acres, North of the ball ground. A fine flock of sheep is pastured here, and is in charge of a knowing "colley," or sheep-dog. Usually on Saturdays, visitors are permitted to roam over the grass.

The Lake lies near the center of the Park, adjoining the Terrace, and covers an area of 20 acres. It is one of the most attractive features of the Park. In summer its wooded and flowery banks afford delightful promenades or resting places, while the beautiful boats of various kinds furnish enjoyment for thousands. At one point it is crossed by a rustic bridge, on which visitors are always standing to watch the boats go by. In winter, when ice has formed of sufficient thickness, the Lake is opened for skaters, for whose safety and comfort every provision is made by the authorities. Then its surface is a sight to see. Such skill and want of skill! such grace and utter lack of grace! are probably exhibited nowhere else in the world on the same space. Old and young—rich and poor—join in the carnival, and it is hard to decide which has the most enjoyment, the crowd upon the ice, or the crowd looking on from the shores.

SHEEP AND LAMBS

63

WINTER SCENE
in CENTRAL PARK.
N.Y.

44

GOAT CARRIAGE.

PELICANS.

DONKEYS.

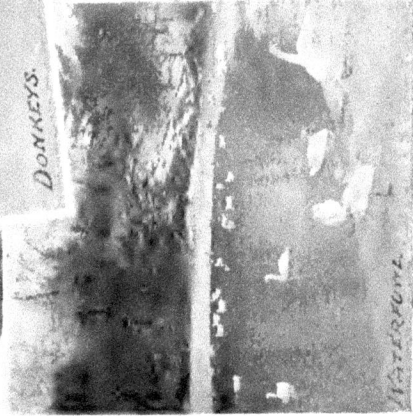

WATERFOWL.

The Pond is near the entrance at 59th St. and 5th Ave., and covers about 5 acres. Around it are some bold and picturesque rocks that materially enhance its attractiveness. The Lohengrin boats upon it are very beautiful, and deservedly popular.

Conservatory Water covers 2½ acres, not far from the 72d St. and 5th Ave. entrance. It is used principally by children for miniature boat races.

The Pool, near the entrance at 8th Ave. and 100th St., is a beautifully shaded retreat. **Harlem Meer,** in the Northeastern corner of the Park, covers over 12 acres, and by many is considered the most romantic of all the Park waters. Near it are the large greenhouses, used in propagating plants and flowers for the ornamentation of the Park.

The Loch covers only an acre, and is not far from the Pool.

Lily Pond is an irregularly shaped pool 200 feet long, with natural grassy shores, shaded at one end by a weeping willow. In this pond are successfully cultivated many varieties of choice water-lilies, including the Egyptian lotus, the purple and red tropical Zanzibar lilies, the deep red Indian lily (*Nymphœa rubra*), the pure white N. dentata and the American yellow lotus and rose-colored Cape Cod lily. These, with other water plants, such as the Papyrus, the strange, unique floating plant Pontederia, or Water Hyacinth, with flowers like an orchid, and the attractive little yellow water poppy, make one of the most unique collections of the kind in the country. In other parts of the Park collections similar to the above may be found. They are specially noteworthy at the Loch and at the Southwest corner of the Harlem Meer, in both of which spots great masses of the Egyptian lotus (*Nelumbium speciosum*) present a most picturesque appearance. At the Bethesda Fountain, a general collection of lotuses and lilies are effective.

VIEW ON LAKE

MAYPARTIES

49

Statues and Monuments in the Park.

Beethoven.—A bronze bust of Beethoven on a granite pedestal 15 feet high, on East side of the Mall, near the Music Stand, unveiled July 22, 1884.

Bolivar.—An equestrian statue of Gen. Simon Bolivar, the Liberator, stands at the West side of the Park, near 81st St. entrance. It is by R. De la Cora, and was a gift from the people and government of Venezuela. It was unveiled June 17, 1884.

Burns.—A bronze statue of Robert Burns, modeled by John Steele, of Edinburgh, was presented to New York by resident Scotchmen in 1880. It stands opposite the statue of Scott, at the Southern end of the Mall.

Columbus.—A granite monument to Christopher Columbus, by Gaetano Russo, was presented to New York by Italian residents in 1893. It stands in the circle near the 8th Ave. and 59th St. entrance. There is also a marble statue of Christopher Columbus, of colossal size, the work of Miss Emma Stebbins, presented to the city by the late Marshall O. Roberts in 1869. Located in McGown's Pass Tavern.

"Commerce," an ideal figure cast in bronze, about 8 feet high, presented to the city in 1865 by Mr. Stephen B. Guion, stands near the 8th Ave. and 59th St. entrance.

Eagles and Goat.—A bronze casting, East of the Mall, executed by Fratin, and presented to the city by Gordon W. Burnham in May, 1863.

Falconer.—A bronze group placed on a high bluff, near the statue of Webster. It was presented by Mr. Geo. Kemp, February 28, 1872, and is the work of George Simonds.

Halleck.—A bronze statue of the poet Fitz-Greene Hallcck was erected on the Mall in 1877. The figure is seated, and placed on a granite pedestal. Modeled by Wilson MacDonald.

Hamilton.—A granite statue of Alexander Hamilton, presented to the city by his son, John C. Hamilton, in 1880. It was executed by. Ch. Conradts, and stands on the West side of the East Drive, N. W. of the Art Museum.

Humboldt.—A bronze bust of Alexander von Humboldt, by Gustave Blaeser, stands on a granite pedestal near the 5th Ave. and 59th St. entrance. It was presented to the city by a number of German residents on the 100th anniversary of the birth of the distinguished savant, September 14, 1869.

"Indian Hunter."—An ideal figure, life-size, in bronze, by Mr. J. Q. A. Ward, stands near lower entrance to the Mall.

Mazzini.—A bronze bust of the Italian agitator, of heroic size, on a pedestal 10 ft. in height, stands on the West Drive, near the Seventh Regiment monument. It is by Turini, and was presented to the city by Italian residents in 1878.

Moore.—On the banks of the Pond, and near the 5th Ave. entrance, is a bust of Thomas Moore, by Dennis B. Sheehan. It was given to the city, May 28, 1880, by the Moore Memorial Committee.

Morse.—A life-size bronze statue of Prof. S. F. B. Morse, by Byron M. Pickett, stands near the 5th Ave. and 72d St. entrance. It was erected by the telegraphic craft in 1871.

Schiller.—A bronze bust of the poet, stands on a sandstone pedestal in the Ramble. It is by C. L. Richter, and was presented by German residents in 1859.

THE LOVERS WALK.

Scott.—A copy of the bronze statue of Sir Walter Scott, modeled by John Steele, and standing in Edinburgh, was presented to New York by resident Scotchmen, in 1872. It is placed on an Aberdeen granite pedestal, on the Mall, near the Southern end.

Seventh Regiment.—A bronze figure of a private soldier of this regiment, modeled by J. Q. A. Ward, was erected in 1874, in commemoration of those members who fell in battle during the late civil war, on the West Drive near 72d St.

Shakespeare.—The bronze statue of William Shakespeare at the lower end of the Mall, was placed in position May 23, 1872, on the 300th anniversary of the great dramatist's birth. It is the work of Mr. J. Q. A. Ward.

The Pilgrim.—This is a bronze statue, 9 ft. high, by J. Q. A. Ward, to commemorate the landing of the Pilgrims on Plymouth Rock, in 1620. The costume is historically correct, and the statue is very picturesque. It is located near the Lake, where the roadway leading from 5th Ave. at 72d St. crosses the Eastern Drive, and is a gift from the New England Society.

"The Still Hunt," by Kemeys, represents a beast of prey ready to leap upon its victim. It is on a rock overlooking the East Drive, near the Obelisk.

Tigress and Young.—A fine group, presented to the Park in October, 1867, by twelve New York gentlemen. It is in bronze, is by Augustus Caine, and stands a few yards West of the Terrace.

Webster.—A bronze statue of Daniel Webster at the junction of the 72d St. and the West Drive. It is the gift of Mr. Gordon W. Burnham, and was modeled by Mr. Thomas Ball.